History of the Early Settlement of Bowmanville and Vicinity

John T. Coleman

BIBLIOLIFE

HISTORY

OF THE

EARLY SETTLEMEN'

O F

BOWMANVILLE

AND VICINITY.

BY J. T. COLEMAN.

RICE · · THIRTY CEN

BOWMANVILLE:

WEST DURHAM STEAM PRINTING AND PUBLISHING HOUSE.

1875.

EARLY HISTORY OF SETTLERS.

N THE early history of Darlington, we find that Mr. John Burk, John W Trull, and Roger Conat, were the pioneers, and first settlers of this Township. They emigrated together, with their families, from the United States to Canada, in the year 1794, and on the 2nd day of October, they landed from their boats on the beach of Lake Ontario, one mile west of Barber's Creek, now Port Darlington.

They were induced to come to this country, by a proclamation issued by Colonel John Greaves Simcoe, (then 'Lieutenant-Governor of Canada), that all males of the age of 18 years, who settled in the country, should be entitled to two hundred acres of land.

In their journey from the Susquehannah River, their former home, they met with innumerable difficulties, and many hardships. Their families and effects were placed on board a Batteau (a large n de boat), which was coasted around the head of the lake, running into bays and inlets, in order to avoid storms, or for the purpose of cooking their meals, and camping during the night ; while the stock, which consisted of two cows and one horse, were driven around the shore on foot, having to cross swamps, marshes, lagoons, outlets, and rivers, as best they could. Those in charge of the boats, having crossed the Niagara river into Canada, were received with great kindness by the Governor, who sent a man

back to assist in bringing around the stock as far as York, now
Toronto. In an extract from a letter written to the Hon Harvey
Burk, I find that his uncle, Jessia Burk, was one of the persons
then engaged in driving this stock. He says, in his letter, " I was
fourteen years and one month old, when we landed in Darlington.
I came all the way on foot, and helped to drive the cattle with
one Tom ———, who lived with the Trull's. When we came to
Big Bay, I was to swim the three year-old colt, belonging to old
Conat, and Tom said, he could swim across. We waited until
the cattle got safely over; I then, being on the colt, put forward,
and soon came to where there was a short break off into deep
water, and the colt went down, clear under , I saw that he
could not swim with me on his back, so I placed my left foot
against his side, and shot myself clear from him. We came ashore
again, and went around the head of the bay, where we found the
cattle on the beach. After surmounting numerous obstacles and
delays, this small band of emigrants reached their destination in
safety." They were surrounded by a primeval forest, the only
human inhabitant being the rude, savage Indian, who looked with
jealous eyes upon the encroachment of the whites.

Landed in a new and wild country, and winter fast approaching, the people comprising this settlement set at once to work, to
construct log shanties, which were plastered on the inside with
mud, and had bark covering for a roof. Mr. John Burk built his
house on the bank of the lake, being the southern portion of the
farm, now owned by his grandson, Wm. K. Burk. In another
extract from the letter, before quoted, Mr. Jessia Burk says : " We
had no neighbors but the Indians for two or three years, save old
Benj. Wilson, and the Trulls, who lived at Baldwin's Creek.
There was not a house within thirty miles to the west, save an old
French trading house, that Wilson got in, and old Conat's, two
miles to the east of Wilson's , and none east of us, short of Smith's
Creek," (Port Hope.) During the winter, these pioneers spent
most of their time in trapping and hunting ; the deer and bear
being so plentiful, that an abundance of animal food could be
procured with but very little trouble. The furred animals were
also very numerous, and required but little skill to trap them, their

skins being about the only thing that could be sold for money
A very great inconvenience felt among them, was the want of
a mill to grind their grain and corn, the nearest being Myer's
Mill, situate at the foot of Lake Ontario, 60 miles distant. Those
who went to mill, usually took two weeks to go and return, using
a canoe for the purpose, and hauling it up on the shore at night,
when a storm occurred, they were weather-bound until it passed
over. On their arrival at the mill, they waited till the grist was
ground, when they returned home in the same manner. As going
to mill was no light undertaking, and attended with so many obstacles and perils, a great many expedients were resorted to, in
order to obviate this necessity. Some of the settlers had brought
large coffee-mills with them, and these were used to grind or crack
their grain. Other contrivances were improvised, one method
very much in vogue, was to make a rude mortar, by hollowing
out a stump; sometimes this was done by boring, or chiseling,
but it was frequently burnt out, and the cavity scraped with a
knife, or other instrument, until all the charred spots were removed; then they had a wooden pounder attached to a swing-pole
They put the corn into the cavity, and pounded it with this rude
pestle. This bruised corn was known by the name of Samp, and
when pounded fine, was made into Johnny Cake, the coarse being
boiled into mush. Another nutritious and wholesome article
of food, was found in the wild rice. which grew in most of the
marshes, and in great abundance at Rice Lake This was first
parched, and afterwards pounded, and either made into cakes, or
boiled, and acted as a healthful absorbent, when taken with animal food.

The Indians were very troublesome. and caused considerable
anxiety, being armed and equipped, and very different from the
remnants of the broken tribes occasionally seen at the present
time Capt. John Trull relates an incident which occurred at this
time in his father's house, when he was a boy. His father was
absent, having gone to Myer's mill, when a squaw, with four pap-
ooses, came to the house, and asked his mother for *nak-paw-nee*
(Flour.) That article being extremely scarce, his mother refused
giving her any; the squaw then searched through the house, and
found the flour in a kneading trough She brought it forth, and

commenced to divide it equally to every one in the room, by giving a double handful to each, beginning with his mother, then to herself, and to each white child, and papoose, until it was all divided, when she took her share in a bag, and travelled off through the woods

Open hostilities were, as a general thing, avoided, and there is only one instance recorded of a white man being killed by the Indians, although most of the settlers were in considerable dread of them. There was, according to their history, one man (Mr. Jno. Burk) among them, who did not share this timidity, but showed a bold front, and when any of them attempted to take liberties, would resent by giving them a sound thrashing   According to all accounts, he did not require much provocation to do so, but the chastising of an Indian by him was looked upon as a pleasant duty, which he was willing to perform on any occasion. For this particular trait of character, the Indians applied a *sobriquet*, to designate him from the rest of the settlers, which was not very flattering.

Mr. Timothy Soper is another of the very early settlers in the Township of Darlington   His father, Mr. Leonard Soper, was born in 1762, and emigrated to Canada in 1788.   The following year, the present Timothy Soper was born in the Township of Sidney, near the head of the Bay of Quinte, and was the first white child born in that Township   At that time, there was no white settlement in this portion of Canada, and only one vessel, the *Mohawk*, a schooner employed in the interests of the North West Fur Company, on Lake Ontario.   Mr. Soper, who, in 1795 removed to the Township of Hope, says, "there was no mill at Smith's Creek, (Port Hope) ; my father went once to Kingston, and several times to Napanee, taking his grist in a canoe."

While living in Hope, Mr. Soper lost a span of horses.   They were gone one year and three months, when he learned from the Indians where they were, and upon repairing to the place, found the horse, and a colt which had been foaled ; the mare was never found.

The first Court of Queen's Bench that ever assembled in the Counties of Northumberland and Durham, was held in a barn, on the premises of Mr. Soper, in Hope, on which occasion, the Judge, (Major MacGregor Rogers,) lawyers, and other officials, chose sides, and played a game of ball, to determine who should pay the expense of a dinner Ephriam Gifford, father of the late Garner Gifford, acted as constable.

Mr. Leonard Soper moved to Darlington in 1805, and erected the first saw mill built in the Township ; but it was burnt down the following year, another was put up near the same place. About this time, Mr. John Burke built a saw mill, on Barber's Creek, from which time the place was known as Darlington Mills until 1823, when it was changed to its present name, (Bowmanville).

In 1806, Mr. Soper purchased from Augustus Barber, (after whom the Bowmanville Creek was named) the present Soper mill property. Mr. Timothy Soper relates an incident which occurred to him some time after his father had built the mill. While engaged in cleaning some fish one morning, a bear came up and commenced feeding upon the offals. Not content with this, she began to feed upon the fish. Mr. Soper called for some one to bring him a gun. One was soon brought, which he discharged at the bear, but being only loaded with light shot, did not kill, but severely wounded her, whereupon she climbed a tree. A heavier charge dispatched her.

Mr. Timothy Soper is now in his 86th year, enjoys good health, and has lived to see every President of the United States take their seats.

In Clarke, Mr. Richard Lovekin was the first settler. He, with others, left Ireland in the 21st of September, 1795, sailing from the cove of Cork. They met with adverse winds, which took them far out of their course, and after a tedious journey, landed in St. Bartholemew, on the 26th of January, 1796, and arrived in New York, 9th of April following. Mr. Lovekin proceeded in advance of his family, with two hired assistants, to locate his land, and prepare a home for their reception. After meeting with numerous adventures, incident to a new and wild country, he settled at the mouth of what was afterwards known as Baldwin's Creek, Wilmot's), where he, after building a temporary shanty, commenced to clear some land, and cut timber for the construction of a house.

Soon after his arrival, himself and men took the boat one evening, and ran up the marsh for the purpose of cutting grass, with which to make their beds. While so engaged, they heard the wolves howling around them, which, at first, the men began to mimic, but the noise continuing, and the wolves increasing in numbers, became so bold as to approach within a short distance of them; the men got frightened, and pulled for the outlet. As they passed along into the lake, the wolves, thirty or forty in number, ranged themselves on each side of the sand-bank, snapping and howling like a lot of furies, to see them escape. After arriving at their shanty, they did not think proper to land until they had seen the last of the dusky forms retire in the shade of the woods; whereupon, they repaired to the shanty, and kept up a large fire the remaining part of the night.

Having, during the summer, cleared some of the land, and constructed and completed a house, with the exception of the doors and windows, Mr Lovekin thought of returning to his family, and, on the following spring, to bring them to their new home. He had about a hundred and fifty dollars in silver, with him, which, on account of its weight, he thought unnecessary to take back, so he concluded to place it in a hollow tree; and for that purpose, wrapped it in paper, put it in a stocking, and securing it with a strong cord, hung it up in a hollow tree, which he had selected, and left the place On his arrival the following year, with his family, he was somewhat astonished, on entering his house, to find it already occupied by an old bear, who rushed down stairs, without ceremony, and jumped through the window On inspecting the house, it was found, from the quantity of leaves and brush piled up in a corner of the room, that the bear had taken up its winter quarters there.

After having, in a manner, settled his effects and family in the house, he went to the tree to see if the money was all safe. He found a small piece of the string, which had been secured to a knotty protuberance within the hollow, but the stocking, and its contents, was gone from where he had placed it. He felt disappointed, and considered it lost; but occasionally it would revert to his mind that he was not sure of this, and so, some time afterwards, to satisfy himself, he set to work and cut down the tree, at the bottom of which, he found portions of the paper, and stocking, cut up fine, and mixed with grass and leaves, which formed a wood-mouse's nest. After removing the nest, he found all his money buried in loose, rotten wood, and mould. Mr Lovekin drew his land from the Government, and became a permanent citizen in 1801. He took the oath of allegiance, was appointed Chief Magistrate of the home district, (which embraced the country from Cobourg to Toronto), and held many offices of trust under the Government. During the war of 1812, he administered the oath of allegiance to many brave and patriotic persons, who took up arms in defence of the country. The following is a form of the oath, and a list of the names of those to whom the oath was administered ·

(AFFIDAVIT.)

County of }
Durham, to Wit. }

Be it remembered, that, before Richard Lovekin, one of His Majesty's Justices of the Peace for the district of Newcastle, the non-commissioned officers and privates of the first regiment of the Durham Militia, whose names are underwritten, haven taken and subscribed the following oath, as prescribed by the Act of the Provincial Parliament, passed the fifth day of August, in the fifty-second year of His Majesty's Reign, entitled an Act "to repeal part of the laws now in force for the training and warning the Militia of the Province, and to make further provision for the raising and training of the said Militia." and which oath has been duly administered to the said non-commissioned officers and privates in obedience to the order of His Honor, Major General Shraffe, President administering the Government of the Province of Upper Canada, communicated through Major General Shaw, Adjutant General of Militia, to William Warren Baldwin, the Lieutenant-Colonel Commanding the said first Regiment of the Durham Militia.

(OATH.)

I do sincerely promise and swear, that I will be faithful and bear true allegiance to His Majesty King George, and him will defend to the utmost of my power, against all traitorous conspiracies and attempts whatever which shall be made against his person, crown, or dignity, and I will do my utmost endeavor to disclose and make known to His Majesty, his heirs and successors, all treasons and traitorous conspiracies and attempts, which I shall know to be against him or them—So help me God.

MILITIA ROLL CALL FOR 1812, BY R LOVEKIN.

Ebenezer Hartwell, Daniel Lightheart, Norris Carr, Augustus Barber, Waterman A. Spencer, James Burke, Nathan Pratt, Samuel Burk, Enoch Davis, John Trull, John Dingman, William Pickle, Matthew Borland, John Wilson, Eliphalet Conat, Richard Martain, Michael Coffun, David Burk, Jeremiah Conat, Thomas Powers, James Flannigan, David Seron, William Preston, Timothy Johnson, Dyer Moore, James Grant, Reuben Grant, Jr., James Hawkins, Jr., Thomas Hartwell, John Paine, Lanson Soper, Caleb Raymond, Joel Byrns, Jr., William Bebee, Nehemiah Vail, Aaron Hills, John Brown, Nathan Haskell, Joel Byrns, Sr., Jonathan Bedford, Jr., John Odell, Nathan Watson, Alexander W. Ross, Luther McNall, Gershom Orvis, Jered Kimball, Jonathan Rodgers, John Potter, Abraham Bowen, Stadman Bebee, Daniel Wright, Israel Bowen, Daniel Crippin, Dorous Crippin, Luke Smades, Joshua Smades, John Walker, Joseph Barden, Pletiah Soper, James Merrill, John Perry, Adna Bates, Francis Lightfoot, Samuel Marvin, William Carr, William Borland, Jr., Roger B. Wolcott, John Spencer, John Hartwell, Myndert Hanis, Senr., John Burn, Alexander Fletcher, Robert Clark, John D. Smith, Leonard Soper, John Haskill, Samuel W. Marsh, Thomas Gaige, Jeremiah Brittain, Daniel Porter, James Hawkins, Sr., Gardner Gifford, Elias Smith, Jr, Roger Bates, James Stephens, Samuel Gifford, Ezra Gifford, Peter Bice, Christopher Merkley, Josiah Caswell, David Gage, Joel Smades, George Potter, David Bedford, Samuel Willet, David Crippin, Benjamin Preston, Reuben Grant, Sr., Abell Allen, Isaac Hagerman, Justin Johnson, Jeremiah Hays, Hiram Bedford, Joseph Caldwell, Stephen Morse, Benjamin Root, Benjamin Preston, Warren Munson, Edward McReloy, Myndert Harris,Jr., Asa Callendar, Joseph Haskell, James Lee, Zephaniah Sexton, Cornelius Daly, Jonathan Sexton, Zachariah Odell, William Munson, Timothy Haskell, Ephraim Gifford, John Voree, Josiah Wilson, Stephen Bedford.

This oath was administered in pursuance with an Act of Legislature, passed in Lower Canada, empowering the Governor General to embody the whole militia force of the country; also endorsing his army bills to the extent of $1,000,000, and providing for $60,000 per annum, for five years, to maintain the defences of the country.

Just before, and immediately after, the declaration of the war of 1812, by the American Congress, was a period of great peril to the Canadian people, "and required, not only all the skill, bravery, and tactics, of both the civil and military leaders, but also a great portion of the wealth of Canada had to be made available, in order to sustain the country against an invading foe , nor was this all that had to be contended with. Many persons who had lately settled in the country, were from the United States, and naturally retained a warm regard for the American Government, and its institutions ; but from the generous policy of the Governor General, in granting 200 acres of land to all male settlers, in the hour of peril, the majority of these stood firm for the cause of their adopted land, while others required something more than gentle words to induce them to come forward in its defence.

In the correspondence of Colonel Baldwin (who was then on military duty in New York) to his friend, Mr. Richard Lovekin, he repeatedly urges upon him the necessity of requiring all ·persons who had taken government grants of land, to take the oath, saying, that those who refuse to help defend the country, should in fair justice, forfeit their lands, so granted. ˙

This measure, no doubt, had the salutary effect of enabling many to decide promptly, in favor of the Canadian Government. Still, there were a few persons, even in the loyal Township of Darlington, who undertook to shirk the responsibility, by fleeing to the swamps, where they engaged, or pretended to be engaged in the manufacture of baskets and shingles. They were, however, interrupted in these industrial pursuits, brought back, and after being heartily laughed at, joined with their neighbors in the defence of the commonwealth, and afterwards remained honored and respected citizens.

In another letter from Col. Baldwin, in reference to the death of General Brock, which occurred at Queenston heights, he says,
　　　　Dear Richard
I have only time to say that we have gained a most decisive victory over our invaders, though we have deeply to deplore the loss of our brave and worthy General, and Mr. McDonell. It is now supposed, that not less than 400 of the enemy fell, in killed and drowned. There were not more than 700, in regulars, militia and Indians, opposed to 1500. We took upwards of 900 prisoners. I will, at another opportunity, write to you the particulars, but have not time now. God bless you
　　　　　　　　　　　　W. W. BALDWIN.
At the termination of this war, which was settled by treaty, signed at Ghent, on the 24th day of Dec., 1814, the finances

both of Upper and Lower Canada, were very much exhausted. It had, however, the effect of developing to a very high degree, the patriotism and loyalty of the provinces, party spirit was hushed, and the people were cemented together for general good, and the prosperity of the country. Money at this time was very scarce among the settlers, who, as a general thing, only raised produce enough for their own consumption. But neither hard times, or war, appeared to deter them from engaging in matrimony, as may be seen from the following, taken from the marriage record of this early period. (I might here say, for the benefit of those wishing to see the original register, that it is in the keeping of Mr. James P. Lovekin, of Clarke.)

Third March, 1807, married, Thomas Conat, of Darlington, to Hannah Stoner   Present, Peter Stoner, her father, Abel Conat, Polly, his wife, and Phœbe Lightheart.

Twenty-first April, 1807, married, John Carr, of Darlington, to Betsey Woodruff, of Pickering, with the written consent of her father.   Present, Norris Carr and wife, James Burk and wife, and Mr. Woodruff's son.

Twenty-eighth December, 1807, married, John Burk, Junior, of Darlington, to Jane Brisbin, of Whitby, with the consent of her sister and brother-in-law.   Present, John Burk, Senr., David Stevens, and David Burk.

Third October, 1811, married, William Pickel, of Darlington, to Nancy Wilson, of Whitby, being first duly published, in presence of William Smith, and Waterman A. Spencer, &c.. &c.

Twenty-eighth October, 1811, married, James Bates, of Clarke, to Elizabeth Burk, of Darlington, in piesence of John Burk, Sr., her father, David Stephens, Jessia Burk, Adna Bates, and Stoddard Bates

Sixteenth June, 1805, married, Luke Burk, of Darlington, to Nancy McBane.   Present, James Burk, John Hartrode, Francis Lightheart, and Rachel Lightheart

Fourth March, 1817, married, Icabod Hodge, to Elizabeth Coolley, both of the Township of Whitby, being first published by Alexander Fletcher, Esq., in presence of Francis Lightheart. of Darlington, William Maxson, and John Stevens, of Whitby.

In speaking of the scarcity of money among the early settlers, the present Mr Richard Lovekin narrates an incident which oc-

curred soon after the war.   Being a young man, he had to go to
Smith's Creek to answer the Roll Call on training day, the 4th of
June, and concluded to take a pack of furs, these being the only
commodity for money, with him.   It was a very hot day, and as
he trudged along, with his pack on his back, thinking of this primitive mode of transporting fur, his reflections upon the products
of the country, military operations, and things in general, were
not of the most gratifying nature.   He was not sure whether he
could reach there in time to answer his name, without abandon-
ing his pack.   However, he finally reached Smith's Creek, covered with perspiration, and very much fatigued.   Having performed
his military duty, he sold his fur, receiving, amongst the money, a
Doubloon, sixteen-dollar gold coin, which he kept for six or eight
years before he could find a person able to change it.   At last.
this was done by Mr. McIntosh, who came to Darlington and
opened a store, many years afterward.

  Mr. Thomas Lovekin relates an incident that occurred in 1815.
He had invited some friends to a corn husking bee, and upon repairing to the field for that purpose, they surprised an old bear,
who had forestalled them, and was busily husking corn on
his own account.   The party having dogs with them, the can-
ines attacked the bear, and, amid the confusion and uproar, it es-
caped to the woods.   Some of the party gave chase, while others
went for guns.   Mr. Lovekin saw, with some chagrin, that his
husking party was a failure for that night, and determined to have
satisfaction from Bruin ; procuring his rifle, and following through
the woods, he came upon and shot him on the brow of the hill,
where the Bowmanville Cemetery is now situated.   He had the
skin, which was a large one, dressed and made into an overcoat.

  The late Samuel S. Wilmot, of Clarke, settled in this country
at an early date.   He was born in the State of New York, at a
place called the Nine Partners, in the year 1795.   His father,
Lemuel Wilmot, emigrated to the province of New Brunswick,
and there settled with his family   The late Mr. S. S. Wilmot remained with his father until he was 21 years of age, when he migrated to Canada, and settled in York.   He there became acquainted
with the late John Steigman, a German, and surveyor, by profes-

sion.   Mr. Wilmot served his time with him, as a surveyor, and after a time, married his daughter.   He then engaged with him as a chain bearer.   They were employed by the Government to survey the main road leading from Kingston to York.   This road was cut four rods wide, and grubbed two rods, it was constructed by Captain Danforth, and though being the main post road, was a very indifferent one ; during summer, after very heavy rains, it was almost impassable.   The first mail carried over this road was taken on a mule, and arrived every two weeks, from Kingston to Darlington.

On the 3rd of April, 1816, Mr. S S. Wilmot moved from Yonge Street, Toronto, to the Township of Clarke, having purchased 400 acres of land, now known as the Wilmot Homestead, from John Hartwell.   At the time Mr. Wilmot moved to Clarke, the Danforth road was impassable through Clarke and Darlington, in the fall and spring, and good travelling was only found during the winter by sleighs.

In a diary kept by him at the time, the settlers then living on the main road in Darlington, (this does not include persons who lived on the lake shore) were as follows, commencing from the west : Stevens, Thos. Powers, Solomon Tyler, David Stevens, John Burk, Squire Fletcher, and John Borland ; in the Township of Clark, were R. Lovekin. J. P., Avery, Bates, Blair, and Hartwell.   There were no settlers north of the main road, in Clarke or Darlington.   It was a dense, unbroken forest, inhabited only by Indians and wild animals.

The land known as the late Bowman Estate, and which com_ prises the principal site of the town of Bowmanville, was first drawn from Government by Mr. John Burk, who, after having built a grist and saw mill upon it, sold it to a Mr. Purdy , but after a time, it again came into the possession of Mr. Burk, who sold it to Mr. Lewis Lewis, who, in connection with the milling business, opened a store.   This was the first store opened in Darlington.   Mr. Lewis remained in business for four years ; he then sold out to Mr. Charles Bowman.   This appears to have been about the year 1824. . The Post Office was located at Black's Hill, (the late Youal Homestead, now occupied by A. Scott)

Col. James Black, Postmaster. It was opened soon after the war of 1812. The mail was brought from Kingston to York, once a week, on mule-back, or when travelling was good, during winter, in a sleigh. Wm. McMullen was mail carrier. His mule, it is said, on good authority, died about twelve years ago in Markham. A Post Office was established at Darlington Mills, in 1829, the late Mr. Robert Fairbairn, then in charge of the Bowman business, being appointed Postmaster. His house was situated on the east bank of the millpond, where an old orchard may now be seen. This orchard he planted soon after his arrival in Darlington. The first mail that came to this place was opened by John Simpson, (the present Hon.) a young man, who was then clerk for Mr. Fairbairn. The mail was carried in an open wagon, with passengers, the passengers usually sitting in the wagon while the mail was changed, it being passed through an open window for that purpose. On one occasion, it is said, the mail came through without the ceremony of having the windows opened, taking the glass and some of the sash along with it. I do not know the precise time that this occurred, but the late Mr. Wm. Glover was then mail carrier. The first person who contracted to deliver the mails at Darlington Mills, was a Mr. Odgen, of Clarke. About this time, Mr Simpson took the census of Darlington, which amounted to 118 persons ; only one house was then erected north of the main road.

Mr. Fairbairn, after retiring from the Bowman business, was succeeded by Mr. John Lester, who conducted the affairs of the firm for five or six years, and then went into business for himself, on the hill, west of the creek.

Mr. Geo. Smart next took charge of the Bowman Estate, and business, and about a year afterwards was accidently thrown from a horse and killed. After Mr. Smart's death, Mr. John Simpson, then a young man eighteen years of age, took upon himself the responsibility of transacting the business of the firm. The business of Bowman & Co., now extended in proportion to the increase of the population, and from the generous system adopted by them in their business relation towards farmers generally, but more especially to those, who, with limited means, had lately arrived to settle in the country. To such as these, the Co. extended an almost unlimited credit, thus affording them the necessary means to prosecute their daily avocations, and agricultural pursuits.   During a long continued business, embracing half a lifetime, this firm rarely or ever, resorted to legal measures to adjust claims.   There are many persons now living, in easy and affluent circumstances, who can trace the foundation of their prosperity to this cause.

In a record, kept by Mrs. David Burke, widow of the late David Burke, of Darlington, it is shown that her ancestors, along with a number of other families, emigrated from Hamburg, Germany, in 1794, under the guidance of a person named Boursey. Instead of taking them to Canada, as he agreed to, he brought them to Genesee Valley, N. Y., where they remained two years, before making the discovery that it was not British territory. Be ing dissatisfied, they then applied to Gov. Simcoe, who gave them grants of land in Markham, and compelled Mr. Boursey to fulfil his agreement. He conveyed them by ox-sleighs, during winter, around the lake

In 1841, the principal part of the village was on the west side of the creek :—A large hotel, two or three stores, a blacksmith shop, cabinet shop, and several fine residences. Had the adjoining real estate been put into the market, the town would, in all probability, have been built on that site.

One of the customs very much in vogue, was the *Charivari.* On the occasion of a wedding, the young men of the neighborhood, provided with horns, bells, tin-pans, &c , &c., always made their appearance, *a la masque* This custom first originated in the French rural districts, and it is probable that, at first, it was productive of more good than harm, as it was only resorted to when public decency was considered to have been outraged, through some ill-chosen or disgraceful match. But this feature in charivari companies was soon lost sight of, after its introduction into the upper province. No distinction was made between a wedding, every way proper and unimpeachable, or one of an opposite character. Many of these demonstrations were indulged in by the early settlers, and there are many holding honorable positions among us to-day, who will remember, with regret, the part they took in them.

One of these charavaris occurred on the occasion of the mar-

riage of Mr. T—— to Miss H——. Nothing was objection-
able in this match, but the company assembled in considerable
force, and after having demanded the fee, which was refused, proceeded in the usual manner to make as much noise and confusion
as possible. The married couple were located in a house, the
upper portion of which was unfinished. The doors and windows
below had been bolted, and barricaded, but the windows in the
upper story had not yet been put in. Some of the company soon
perceived this, and climbing up, entered through the window;
they then found their way down stairs, unfastened the door, and
let in the crowd, who rushed into the room occupied by the bride
and bridegroom, laid hold of Mr. T——, and brought him, *en-
deshabille*, to the street, where they placed him on a rail, with the
intention of giving him a free ride. He then consented to com-
ply with the rules of the company. The money being in the possession of his wife, he asked permission to go to her room to get
it, which request was granted. In the meantime, some of the
party, with a view of rendering his appearance as ridiculous as
possible, had blackened his face with lamp-black; but his mind
was so much occupied with other matters, that he did not think
of this, and when released, hurried to his wife's apartment, and,
in a hasty and confused manner, demanded the amount. The
lady, whose natural amiability of character had given away to one
of hostile feeling, did not recognize her husband in his changed
appearance. She seized a brass candlestick, and dealt him a blow
over the eye, which produced a very ugly flesh-wound, causing the
blood to run freely. and placed herself in an attitude to repeat the
blow; he shouted to her not to strike him again—that he was her
husband, her dear William. Aware of what she had done, she
expressed her regrets in the most piteous tones—took him in her
arms, kissed him, and called him by the most endearing names;
the whole forming one of the most affecting scenes, probably, ever
witnessed by a charavari company.

A case of practical joking is related of two old residents, one
of whom is still living in Bowmanville. Mr. G—— who had been
out shooting, observed Mr. S—— standing near a field, in which
a horse was quietly grazing. Having first loaded his gun with a

heavy charge of buck shot, he approached Mr. S——, who inquir-
ed what luck he had met with.   He replied, that there was plenty
of game, but his fowling piece was so weak in the breech, that
she would scarcely kill.   For instance, said he, " I will bet you
the liquor, you cannot make that horse look up, or even wink, by
shooting at him from here.   " Done," said Mr. S— ;," Give me
the gun;" whereupon the gun was handed to him, and after taking good aim, he fired.   It made a terrific report, the recoil of
the gun sending him to the right about ; the horse ran a short
distance, and dropped dead.   Mr. G—— said," You have won
the liquor, I will pay for the whiskey, and you pay for the horse."
This story can be vouched for by many residents, and the owner
of the horse, Mr. Thomas Hall.

There was a certain class among the old settlers of Bowmanville
that had a keen relish for fun.   Some of them had such a high ap-
preciation of a good joke, that they considered it one of the best
of human attributes to be able to take a joke, as well as to give it
On one occasion, a choice lot of these spirits met in the old dis-
tillery to discuss passing events, and to while away a few fleeting
hours in convivial pleasantries.   One of their associates, Mr. G.,
was absent that evening, having gone down the creek to spear
salmon.   It was a usual thing at those primitive gatherings, to
wind up the evening's doings with a collation of some kind, improvised for the occasion ; in consequence of which, dark hints
had been frequently thrown out about hen-roosts being denuded,
and duck-pens visited , but whether there was any truthful foun-
dations for these insinuations, will now, most likely, ever remain
doubtful ; but there is not the slightest doubt that, if poultry of
any kind had ever found their way in there, the red-hot furnace
afforded one of the most commodious and expeditious places
known for cooking them.   On this occasion, some of the parties
present conceived the idea that, as Mr. G—— was the owner of
a very fine gobbler, it should, for the present, be sacrificed to ap-
pease the cravings of appetite ; and, in order not to steal it, they
concluded to take the turkey, have it cooked, and then invite Mr.
G—— to help them eat it, as he would most likely be very hungry after fishing.   About midnight, he returned, and was agree-

ably surprised when he received the invitation to come and take lunch with a few friends, to which he readily assented.

On joining his friends, he beheld a sight fit to tempt an epicure, and enough to make a hungry man's mouth water. A splendid roast turkey was laid out on the board, with trimmings and extras, and something hot to wash it down. He pronounced the affair a capital get-up, and the whole thing a complete success. His friends intimated that as he was absent in the fore part of the evening, and therefore not responsible for anything that had been done, he should give his word of honor, to keep mum on the subject. With feelings of wounded pride, at their seeming lack of confidence, he said he most assuredly would.

Everything being thus satisfactorily settled, and supper waiting, they requested him to take the head of the table, and do the carving, which he did in a very creditable manner. Meanwhile, the party, after discussing the merits and demerits of the gobbler, his live weight, dead weight, probable age, and by whom he was raised, became so pointed in their remarks, as to leave very little doubt on Mr. G.'s mind, as to who was the owner of the turkey. He immediately arose, and said, " You are a set of scoundrels ; I believe you have taken my turkey," to which they replied, " Yes, we have ; but you gave your word of honor to be mum." " Gentlemen," said Mr. G., after a few moments' reflection, " I am sold, but don't let this interfere with the enjoyment of our supper."

MORMONS.

In 1839, Bowmanville was visited by Mormon delegates, holding forth great inducements to converts, to follow them to the land of promise, situated somewhere in the United States. The Mormon interests were represented by Messrs. Babit and Taylor. The former, in one of his lectures, (which was largely attended, and in which some of the farmers began to take a very great interest) tried to establish, by comparison of the Hebrew and Indian languages, that the Indians of America were the descendants of the ten lost tribes of Israel. Having concluded his lecture, he asked if any one present could controvert the position taken by him. Whereupon the Rev. Mr. Tapscot, Baptist minister, arose and asked him, whether or not, it was essential for a person endeavoring to establish such a point, to possess a knowledge of the

Hebrew language, to which Mr. Babit replied, that it was.   Mr. Tapscot then asked him if he possessed a knowledge of that language ; he replied that he did to a certain extent.   After being questioned for sometime, and showing total ignorance in reference to the subject, he tried to excuse himself by saying that, being on a journey, and not able to refer to his books, he was not so well posted as he otherwise should have been.   Mr. Tapscot then remarked, that however limited a person's knowledge of a language might be, they very rarelyforgot the alphabet, and asked him if he could repeat it, or tell him the first letter of it , which he was forced to acknowledge he could not, and with confusion and chagrin, he saw the tables turned against him, and himself and colleague, exposed as false prophets and humbugs. They soon left the town.   Thus ended disastrously the first attempt to establish Mormonism in Bowmanville

BURIAL PLACES OF EARLY SETTLERS.

Of the Burial places of early settlers, many occur along the shore of Lake Ontario.   One of the first places of interment in this Township, was at Port Darlington, a little to the South of Peter Hambly's house.   Indians, as well as whites, were there buried.   Most of the latter were afterwards removed, but while Mr. Dillon was engaged some years ago in building, and grading the wharf road, human remains, in considerable quantities, were brought to the surface.

A similar place was known to have existed on the Base Line, near the rise of ground west of the quarry.   Mr. W. K. Burk relates an instance of a man, and wife, who were buried on a farm near the lake shore, and twice, during his younger days, he fixed the palings around their graves.   Years ago these had disappeared, and the precise place of the graves can no longer be traced, as the whole field has for many years been under a state of cultivation.

Those facts show the necessity and propriety of establishing public burial places, in the form of Cemeteries, the ground of which cannot afterwards be controverted, or applied to other uses.

INDIAN BURIAL PLACES.

Of burial places, or repositories for the dead of the aborigines. several have, from time to time, been discovered throughout the country. Soon after the settlement of the Township of Manvers, one was discovered on Lot No. 3, 11th Con., situated on a pro montory of high table-land, which projected out in the form of a pear, elevated about forty feet above the flat swamp, by which it was partly surrounded. On the top of this place was a depression of about six feet, in which the Indian remains were found buried, from five to six feet below the surface. This was the condition in which it was found in 1839, by Mr Jas P. Lovekin, Mr. John Wilmot, and others, at which time there were two trees growing in the soil that covered the bones.

Among all classes of Indians, these places are held in great veneration, and by them are never disturbed. This, however, is not the case with the white men ; some of whom visit these places for the laudable purpose of gaining knowledge, that might tend to inform us of their curious habits, customs of life, and past history, while others go from mere idle and wanton motives, and desecrate them, by mutilating and carrying off large quantities of the re-mains, for no other purpose than, after satisfying their vulgar cu-riosity, to be thrown carelessly aside ; thus, they are either lost or destroyed. This has, undoubtedly, been the case with the one in Manvers, which, from its size and general character, would indi-cate that a large number had been buried there. It cannot now, without difficulty, be determined, whether this has been an ordi-nary place of burial, or whether they are the remains of those who have fallen in battle. In the former case, it is usual to find the bones laid in some usual form, while in the latter, they are found heaped and thrown together, promiscuously. As, in their primi-tive mode of warfare, tomahawks and war-clubs were commonly used, a number of indentures and fractures may be traced upon the craniums, produced by scalp wounds received in their hand to hand conflicts.

Another of these places of interment is found at Ball Point, Scugog (Indian, crooked devil) Lake. For a long time after its discovery, it bore the reputation of containing the remains of a gigantic race. The truth of this, however, is not borne out by subsequent investigations. All the bones that I have seen from that place, are of the ordinary size. Dr. Reid, a well-known phys-

the Indians, evidently, had his head crushed by a blow ; the other had a hole cut through the base of the brain, and the squaw had been scalped, the skin hanging in wrinkled folds over her brow, while a tomahawk wound, causing a deep gash in her forehead, just above the right eye, had no doubt caused her death.

The different expressions in the countenances of these figures, were finely delineated, and as distinctly portrayed, as if done on canvass by a good artist. The eyebrows, eyes, ears, nose, lips, teeth and chin, were formed by the natural growth of the wood, standing out in bold relief, and by no theory has it ever been satisfactorily explained, how these likenesses have been produced on the living tree. This curiosity is still in the possession of a citizen of Green Bay, who found it growing in the woods, about 10 miles from the city, and who takes pleasure in showing it to visitors.

Over the whole continent of North America, we have evident proof of there once having been a very numerous and powerful people. They are found scattered over the different parts of the country, from the ice bound regions of the Arctic Sea and Coast of Labrador, to the sunny shores of Florida and the Pacific Ocean, and although divided into many tribes, differing from each other in many respects, they are nearly all of the same color, have similar superstitions, and essentially belong to one great family. The extensive Indian mounds found in Wisconsin, and other parts of the United States, show that a great number of people must have been engaged for many years in their construction. But this once numerous family appear from some evolution in nature, to be passing rapidly away.

When Nova Scotia was first discovered, it was inhabited by a tribe of Indians, of mild and pacific deportment, known to the whites as the red Indians, on account of their particularly red color. The tribe then numbered several thousands, but is now totally extinct.

The Indians have many superstitions. One that exists among the Lake Superior Indians, in connection with an Island, known as the Manitou, probably had its origin in the mirage which often occurs during spring and fall, when this island appears to be elevated much above its natural position, and again to be submerged beneath the surface of the lake. This phenomena takes place nearly every night, just before sunset, during the month of June. The Indians believe this island to be inhabited by a Manitou. There are different kinds of Manitous ; some are good, others are bad ; this one they believe to be very wicked, and if an Indian is drowned while out in his canoe, they, in some way, connect it with this Manitou, and no Indian can be persuaded to set foot upon the island, or to go near it. I was informed of this by a Mr. Whitesides, Photographic Artist, who made a tour around Superior, for the purpose of taking stereoscopic views. When approaching the island, having a Mackinac boat, and two assistants, one of them, an Indian, when aware of Mr. Whiteside's intentions, threatened to jump overboard, unless he changed the course of the boat, and put him on the main shore ; nor·could bribes or threats alter the Indian's determination.

ZOOLOGY.

CONCHOLOGY.

The zoology of this portion of Canada has undergone a very material change, since its early settlement, not only relative to the Mammals and Fish, but also to the Birds, Reptiles, and Shells. Among the latter, quite a number of the *Hellicies*, or land snails, have disappeared, as well as several species of the *Unios*, fresh water Muscles, as in the case with *Unios Striatus*, and *U. Gibosus*; these were formerly found, in great plenty, in Soper's Creek, between his mill and the Grand Trunk bridge. The *U. Fragilis*, paper shell Muscle, is found at the mouth of Burk's marsh, and *U. Complimatus*, pink shell Muscles, on the mud shoals, common to all the marshes, and at Scugog Lake. This Muscle, it is well known, forms, during the winter, the principal food of the Musk Rat, and the numbers devoured by a small family in one season, would appear almost incredible ; the empty shells, lying adjacent to their house, would amount to several wagon-loads. There are, in all, about fifteen known species in Canada, one of which is edible. Another species, which was found in the lower St. Lawrence, *U. Margratifera*, was taken in great numbers, on account of a pearl which it supplied ; and at that time, the exportation of this pearl formed quite an important branch of commerce, between Canada and France. The *Lymnias* are still numerous in the ponds and marshes, and they, as well as the *Planorbis*, have been appropriated by the ladies, for the purpose of making ornamental frame-work, and shell baskets. These muscles form a large portion of the food of aquatic birds and fish.

REPTILLIA.—OPHIDIA.

As regards the reptiles, a very popular, but erroneous, impression exists, that some of the snakes and lizards, in our immediate vicinity, are poisonous   With but one exception, there is not a poisonous reptile known in Canada, and even this one is limited to a very small extent of territory.   It is known as *Crotalis Massasauga*, a small rattlesnake, found in the vicinity of Niagara, Hamilton, and some of the most southern portions of Lake Erie.   They have, however, of late years, become very scarce.   The average length of this snake is from two feet six, to three feet.

The family *Crotalis*, comprise a great many species, and are all indigenous to America.   They are very numerous in the Rocky Mountains, California, and Mexico.   While collecting and preserving Natural History specimens, for the University of Kentucky, in 1866, I received a specimen of *Crotalis, C. Adamenteus*, or Diamond Rattlesnake, named from some beautiful yellow diamond markings, which commence at the head, and increase in size with the body, gradually diminishing towards the end of the tail.   This snake, when received, was alive and healthy, and measured seven feet five inches.   When irritated, it threw itself into a coil, with its head and tail erected in the centre, and kept up a continuous rattle.   The regent of the Institution, fearing that some accident might occur, thought it best to have its fangs removed. An apparatus was soon improvised, and after securing its head firmly, we commenced to probe for one of the fangs.   They were four in number, two on each side of the upper jaw, and were folded down in the jaw in a small grove, similar to the closing of a jacknife blade.   While thus engaged, the animal became excited, erected the fang, and began to eject poison from it, something in the manner of jetting liquid from a small syringe.   This was caught in a vessel, and in color and consistency, resembled sweet oil. About a fluid ounce of this virus was preserved for experiments. It is acid to the taste, and perfectly harmless when taken into the mouth, and may be swallowed with impunity.   It is only fatal in its effects, when coming in contact with the blood.   When this occurs, the fluid portion is separated from the glutinous part, and coagulation takes place.   Its action on the blood is similar to lemon juice, or strong vinegar, with fresh milk.   The poison is generated in a ramification of small nerves, situated in the cheek, behind the eye, and conveyed to a small sack at the base of the fang, which has a tube extending through it to the point, which is formed very much like the nib of a pen ; thus, when it strikes its victim, it tears or scratches the bottom of the wound, making a receptacle for the virus. The flesh of these snakes is eaten by the California Indians. At another time, I received a *Crotalis Massasauga*, that had bitten a boy of twelve years of age, who was picking currants in the garden. This boy was bitten in the second toe of the left foot. On being bitten, he called to his mother, who, after killing the snake with a poker, went for a doctor. In the meantime, intense irritation and inflammation were produced, the leg swelling very rapidly. Upon the arrival of the medical man, convulsions had set in, which baffled all medical skill, the boy dying in an hour from the time of his being bitten. The best known remedy for the bite of these snakes, is to partake freely of alcoholic spirits, and if taken immediately after being bitten, no evil consequences follow. Another remedy, in vogue among the hunters and western men, is, (in the absence of spirits) to cut a portion out of the wound, and fill the place with gunpowder, which is at once ignited.

In this portion of Canada, we have no poisonous snakes or reptiles, of any kind. We have four species of snakes, (three Colubers, and one Constrictor) which are all perfectly harmless. *C. Vernalis,* grass snake, which is the most common, and *C. Sirtalis,* also a little one, rather rare, with a ring round its neck, usually not more than five to seven inches in length, and *Bascanion Constrictor,* known here as the black water-snake, common to the marshes, and Scugog Lake.

Snakes are ovoviviparous, producing eggs, containing living animals. From a female *Coluber,* I have taken thirty-six eggs. They were contained in an ovaduct, and separated from each other by the contraction of the egg sack, around the end of each egg, and presented an appearance somewhat similar to a number of short linked sausages. The eggs, on being expelled from the ovaduct, presented a white appearance, and were covered with a tough opaque skin ; they much resembled the egg of the small red mud-turtle. On being cut open, the young snake, about two and a half inches in length, made its appearance, and was capable of crawling about.

VERMES.

A very popular idea exists among many persons, that a horse hair, after remaining for some time in water, will change to a living animal. This, however, is a very great error. The idea, no doubt, originated from the habit of some of the Caddice Worms, which live inside of tubes constructed by themselves, of different materials, such as grains of sand, leaves, bits of wood, straws, and hairs. These worms are common to fresh water streams and ponds ; several of them can be seen together in a still, deep part of our creeks, or springs, with their heads protruding from their portable dwellings, and when disturbed, withdrawing entirely within their tubes.

There are two worms that somewhat resemble a horse-hair—*Gorgius Aquaticus*, and *Tenia Filiaria*—the latter is from three to five inches in length, and, as its name indicates, is of a thread-like appearance. It is parasitic, and frequently found in the muscle and stomach of fish They are very common in the large trout of Lake Superior, and are occasionally found in the White Fish of Lake Ontario, as well as in birds and animals. I have also seen them in springs. This animal belongs to the class of tape worms, and has a sucker-like mouth. The former is much more active, and of various colors, being a dark grey or brown, and sometimes black. It derives its name from being found in knotty masses. In some places, they are very numerous, but I have only observed a few in this locality, and those were near the head of the marsh at Barber's Creek. Either of these worms can be readily distinguished from a horse-hair, containing a Caddice, with its head and fore feet protruding from the base of the hair

Of the turtles, we have two species ; the lesser one is known as the small red, or Box Turtle, the other as the Snapping Turtle. They were both highly esteemed by the Indians, and early settlers, as an article of diet. .

SAURIANS.

The Lizards are not very numerous , probably, half a dozen species may be found in this vicinity. One of these, the smallest, is commonly met with in new chopped fallows, under rotten logs and decayed chips. There are two other species, which are terrestrial, and two others which are aquatic. The largest of the latter, *Menobranchus Lateralis*, known as mud pointer, mud puppy, &c., although common to all the great lakes of North America, is very rarely met with in this immediate neighborhood. I once saw one lying on the lake shore, near Darlington Harbor, in a partial state of decomposition, and another, captured in Toronto Bay, which was preserved, and is now in the Museum of Toronto University. These lizards abound in great numbers on a shoal in Lake Superior, which surrounds Standard Rock, situate forty miles in a south-east direction from the harbor of Marquette. This rock, which is not discernable in rough weather, can readily be seen when the lake is calm , at which time, its summit remains a few feet above the surface. This shoal varies in depth, from three to five feet, and during the spawning season it is frequented by salmon trout, for the purpose of depositing their eggs.

At this season, the bottom of the shoal is literally swarming with these lizards, and the stomachs of those that were taken were gorged with trout spawn. Some of the largest were about a foot in length, and of a dark brown color above, mottled with dark spots ; lightish grey underneath, with a lateral line running along the side, from the head to the tail. This lizard has the gills on the outside, which are erected like two tufts on each side of the head

These animals are held in much dread by the French fishermen, who believe them poisonous, even to the touch, and when one gets fouled in their nets, instead of shaking it loose, or taking it in the hand, as they would a fish or a frog, they invariably cut away the meshes of the net, leaving a large hole to be repaired. Although these fishermen have been acquainted with this lizard for successive generations, and never knew a single instance of any harm resulting from them, this silly superstition still exists amongst them.

CRUSTACEA.

The Craw Fish, small fresh water lobsters, is one of the crustaceous animals, found in our vicinity, and is common in streams throughout the whole of America. When schoolboys, we used to amuse ourselves by putting two of them together, and watch their antics, while engaged in a sort of a grotesque wrestle. These Craw Fish are eaten by many persons, and considered a great delicacy. Trout, and most other kinds of fish, prey upon them. They are also taken by the racoon

There are several species of Leeches which inhabit our marshes, of which the Horse Leech is the largest There are none of them used for medical purposes.

MAMMALIA.

In all the various branches of Natural History, there are none that have undergone a greater change in this country than the rodent animals   Among them are found some of the finest fur-bearing animals known in the world, such as the Otter, Marten, Mink, Ermine, Fisher, and Beaver. In the early history of Canada, those animals abounded in great plenty, furnishing a large supply of pelts, which formed the staple production of the country. Most of these animals have long since become extinct. The Beaver, that noble monarch of the furred tribe. which furnished food and clothing to the Indian, long before the intrusion of the whites on this continent, is, like him, fated to disappear before the advance of civilization. In different parts of the country, we still find their remains, in the form of extensive beaver meadows ; their lodges and dams having long since gone to decay. Having been, for the last two years, in the Lake Superior country, where these animals still exist in considerable numbers, I have had the opportunity of studying the peculiar habits and customs of this extraordinary animal. They display great intelligence in the selection and construction of their habitations, and would almost appear to bring into action, reasoning powers, rather than instinct.

The Bank Beaver, are those which have their abode on large rivers, where a dam can not be constructed   Such is the case with beavers inhabiting the Missouri, Yellowstone, and other large rivers   In their migrations, which occur from scarcity of food, and other causes, they have been known to travel across the country, until a suitable place was found, in which to start a new colony ; this is generally on some small stream

After taking a survey of the premises, and calculating the amount of food it will furnish, they set to work under one who is the sole director, first to build a dam, (none of these beavers ever having seen one built) and cut canals. In the construction of their dams, a great deal of mechanical ingenuity is displayed, and from which some useful lessons in engineering might be taken. No two dams are precisely alike; they vary in form, length, and material, according to the situation, size of stream, or number of beavers to be accommodated. Very frequently, logs are morticed, or dovetailed, together, in order to secure them more firmly in their places; and while some are thus engaged on the dam, others are employed in cutting canals through higher portions of ground that will not be inundated when their dam is finished. These enable them to float logs (after the trees are cut down) from the adjacent points of timber, to various parts of their pond, for the purpose of furnishing themselves with food, and material to build their lodges with. Now, it may be asked, without forethought, consideration, and conclusion, how would the beaver know that this canal, when finished, would be of any practical use or benefit to him. Some of these canals, lately measured by a Mr. Morgan, of Lake Superior, were found to be upwards of seventy yards in length, and were always filled with water, when the dam was completed. It shows plainly, that the beaver, in selecting a place for a new colony, takes into consideration the whole surroundings, calculates the quantity of food, and material, that can be brought into requisition, and after coming to a conclusion, proceeds to utilize it to their own wants and requirements. While in Superior, I received some fine specimens of beaver, one of the largest of which weighed forty-six pounds, although, I believe, they attain a much greater size. The beaver of Canada—*Castor Canadensis*— and the beaver of Hudson Bay—*Castor Fiber*—are identical. They are capable of cutting down trees two or three feet in diameter, the bark of which forms their winter food. They prefer Balm of Gilead, White Poplar, and Birch, but will eat many other kinds. They have a very powerful pair of incisors in each jaw, but the cutting is done with the teeth in the under jaw, turning their head sideways, at right angles with the tree, for that purpose; and after working for an hour, are generally relieved by another beaver. Often, two or more beavers work at the same tree. A beaver will cut down a tree, one foot through, in two hours and a half, and seldom more than one a day.

The flesh of the beaver is very highly esteemed, both by the Indians and white hunters. It has a flavor peculiar to itself, bearing some resemblance to beachnut pork, but more sweet and juicy.

The Indians have several superstitions in connection with the beaver. The Chippewas will, on no occasion, partake of beaver meat until they know that a bone, in one of the fore-legs, is taken out and buried. The cause of this, I have never been able to ascertain, though Jack La Pette, a Chief living with the remnant of his tribe, sixteen miles below Marquette, explained to me a tradition which they believe in, in regard to the creation of the world. He says that, previous to the creation, all was water, and that the Great Manitou made three animals, the Muskrat, Otter, and Beaver, and told the Muskrat to dive down to the bottom, and bring up some mud. He dove, and on coming up, said that he could not find bottom ; whereupon, the Manitou got angry, and changed his tail, which was formerly like the otter's, to an angular shape, and denuded it of fur. He then sent down the otter, who returned, and said that he had found the bottom, but had nothing to carry up dirt in. Then the Manitou made the beaver's tail of a flat oval form, and the animal disappeared beneath the surface, and came up with a quantity of mud on his tail (with which he has carried mud ever since.) This dirt the Manitou took, and with it, created an island, which has been gradually increasing, until it has attained its present size, known to the white man as the terrestial globe.

Beavers, while migrating, are sometimes met with by the Indians, who usually, on such occasions, exterminate the whole lot of them. The bank beaver does not construct lodges, but tunnels the bank of the river. The entrance of the tunnel is always below low water mark, and after running ten or fifteen feet into the bank. extends upwards above water level, often under the roots of a tree, or bottom of a large stone, and near enough to the surface to admit air. Where the roots of a tree are not convenient, they erect a pile of sticks, having first eaten of the bark. These piles of sticks are often found by the Indians, who at once recognize them, and search along the bank for the entrance of the tunnel, where they place a trap. They then remove the sticks, and drive the beaver into the trap.

Another method, very successfully practised by the Indians, is to make a breach in the dam, well knowing that the beaver will turn out, and repair it as quickly as possible. Along this breach the Indians place their traps, in such a manner, that the beaver is sure to be taken, being, through excitement, rendered less wary and watchful. The castoreum of the beaver is contained in two glands, near the Anal Canal. It is of a brownish yellow color, having a strong peculiar odor, and was considered by the ancients to possess strong medical virtues. It is now generally used to decoy animals into traps

The otter, although a few are still found in the wild northern part of Canadian forests, are scarce in all the front Townships. The last that I have seen were in Lake Scugog, about twelve years ago, while engaged in duck shooting, on which occasion three came swimming within gun-shot, I was at this time standing on a piece of bog, below Staley's landing. This animal furnishes a very fine article of fur, but its flesh is never eaten, even by the Indians, being dark, and giving off a very fœtid odour. They are very tractable when young, and make nice pets. One that a squaw brought down the river and sold to a gentleman in Ottawa, was remarkably clever at catching fish. He was sometimes taken in a boat to a place in the river, where the red fin suckers would run in shoals. On approaching them he was always on the alert, and certain to capture some of the first that tempted to pass the boat, apparently enjoying the sport as much as any of the parties present. The principal food of this animal is fish, but they will eat, if occasion requires, all kind of molusks, crawfish, and even carrion.

The Pine Martin, once as plentiful through the country as the squirrels have been of later years, have been exterminated, and are now completely extinct.

The Mink is still very highly esteemed, on account of its fur, and are so prolific, that they still remain in considerable numbers along the creeks and swamps. These animals have from five or six, to eight or nine young at a litter, each season, and in some places in the United States they are propagated in a partially domesticated state, with considerable benefit to those so engaged, and there is not the slightest doubt that their propagation might be conducted on a more advantageous principal in this country, where their fur is of a much superior quality.

ORNITHOLOGY.

The birds of North America have all been described, and written upon, by various authors; and there has been no new species added for a number of years. It is, therefore, supposed that the birds of North America have all been discovered; and in reference to the treatment of this subject, I do not intend to give the individual history, but to treat upon the different groups and families of birds, frequenting our locality, and propose to divide them into three divisions, the first comprising the resident birds, the second, birds that migrate from the north, and the third, consisting of the true migratory birds, that visit our country each year, upon the approach of spring.

The resident birds are those that remain with us the whole year round. Among them are found the Rough Grouse, or Partridge, and the Spruce Partridge. This last named bird is not found in the front townships, but is common in Manvers and the adjoining country north. It is a very unsuspicious creature. and allows itself to be taken very easily, by placing a noose on the end of a light pole, while sitting on the low branches of the spruce tree, which is their favorite place of resort. The Quail, once quite plenty, were also residents, as well as the Hairy and Downey Woodpecker, Nut-hatch, or Sap-sucker, and the Chicadeedee.

These last named birds are never found associating together, save on the approach of winter, after all the other feathered songsters have left, and the forest is denuded of its foliage, and everything wears a dreary and lonely aspect. Birds that are then the sole tenants of the woods, band together in mutual good fellowship, and a company of three or four woodpeckers, half a dozen nuthatchers, with a dozen or twenty chicadeedees, may frequently be seen going through the woods, keeping up a continual and incessant chorus, twittering, chirping, and piping, which contrasts very singularly with the surrounding solitude, that, at this season, pervades the Canadian forests.

The birds that migrate here during winter, are more numerous than the resident birds, and, unlike the true migratory birds, many of them are irregular in their visits, as in the case with the Cross Bills, of which there are two species, the red, and the white-winged. They are quite plenty during some winters, and then are not to be seen again for two or three years. The Snow Bunting is more regular in its migration, and may be seen in large flocks every winter. On the approach of spring, they retire to the far north to breed, their nest and eggs having been found on the coast of Lapland. The Lesser Red Pole, is another winter visitant, and may be seen in flocks, feeding upon the seeds of the different kinds of weeds, left in the gardens and fields. They are a sprightly, active little bird, and appear at a distance to be of a grey color, but on a nearer approach, the male will be observed to have the upper portions of the neck and breast, as well as rump feathers, marked with a rich deep carmine. This is more noticeable towards spring. Its notes somewhat resemble those of the cock yellow-bird, and have led many persons to erroneously suppose them to be the yellow-bird, in its winter plumage, but the migration of the yellow-bird south, during our winter, is so well known, as to preclude any possibility of its being the same.

The Ptarmigan, or white grouse, frequently migrates from the coast of Labrador and Hudson Bay, into the northern range of our Townships. In the year 1862, they came within 15 miles of Ottawa, and were killed in considerable numbers, while feeding upon the willow tops.

The Snowy Owl, one of the largest of this family of birds, and an inhabitant of the Arctic regions, comes here occasionally, during intense cold weather. Their food consists principally of small quadrupeds and grouse, but they are also excellent fishers, and will watch at an open place in the ice on lakes and rivers, for the approach of fish, which they seize with their talons, and devour. The Ptarmigan has a peculiar habit when the weather is intensely cold, of burying themselves in the loose snow, and remaining there until the cold snap is past, when they again emerge from their place of shelter.

The great Cinerous Owl is an occasional winter visitant, but very rarely met with in this part of Canada. Having been for many years collecting birds, and visiting various museums, I have only seen two stuffed specimens, and one live bird. One of the stuffed specimens was sent to the French Exposition, by the Normal School Natural History Department, Toronto. The live bird was captured in Cartwright.

The Jer Falcon is one of the most rare and beautiful of the Hawk family. Only one or two specimens have ever been killed in Darlington. They occasionally come here late in the fall, or early in winter.

The Canada Jay (Perisoreius Canadensis) is another winter visitor. This rather singular bird has some traits of character, peculiarly its own, being readily domesticated, and full of antics. He is known to the shanty-men and trappers, by the name of Whisky Jack, Venison Bird, and Carrion Bird. As soon as he discovers the smoke of a shanty, he is sure to make his appearance, and if any meat, bones, or slops are thrown out, he commences to help himself to whatever comes in his way, and will readily take a piece of meat off the end of a stick, a few feet in length, that is held out to him ; and if a person is carrying a piece of meat on his back, he will not hesitate to alight on it, and eat his fill. One of those birds was brought to me while in Ottawa It had received a slight injury on the tip of the wing, from a gun-shot wound, received about an hour before I placed it in a cage, which it examined very minutely. After a short time, I offered it some meat on the end of a stick, of which he was a little shy, but after a time, he took it, and in an hour from the time he was placed in the cage, it would eat from my hand.   When let out, it would go to the window and catch flies, which it would keep in its mouth until a sufficient quantity was collected, when it would go and deposit them, with a number of other things, in the corner of the cage.   When left to itself, it would bring them all out, look them over, and try to hide them in a more secure place.   While having this bird in my possession, I was presented with a young robin, about half grown, which I put into the cage, and turned the venison bird out ; but it appeared to show such great solicitation on account of the robin, being continually watching it, that I put them both together in the cage, when the venison bird commenced to feed the robin, and continued to do so for many weeks, until the robin could take ample care of himself.   This bird had frequent opportunities to escape, being often on top of the house, but would always return when called.

The true migrating birds are by far the most numerous, and it is by them that our lakes, ponds, rivers, forests, fields, and groves are each year re-animated, on the return of spring. Some of those attract us by their graceful movements, or the beautiful markings of their plumage, while others charm us with the sweetness of their melody.   It is also interesting to watch them while engaged in the construction of their nest, or the feeding of their young. Go where you will, those welcome visitors are constantly engaging our attention.   To give an individual history, or even sketch of each species, would require a much greater space, and more time than I can here devote to it.   I shall therefore merely numerate the birds that are to be found in our own locality, with a few remarks upon some that I think are the least known or understood.

Commencing with the .Hawks, we have about twelve different species ; of the Eagles, two species—the Bald Headed Eagle, and Golden Eagle, one Fish Hawk, eleven species of Owls, and nine varieties of Woodpeckers.

In the early settlement of Canada, a very large woodpecker, which at that time was quite numerous, has not been seen in this Township for the last thirty or forty years, this bird was known to the old settlers by the name of Woodcock, or Logcock.   I first got an account of it from Mr. E. Silver, of this town, several years ago, while being engaged in making a collection or birds.   He

describe it to me as a climber, and also said it was in the habit
of making a loud noise before rain. I having associated the name
of this bird with the true Woodcock, and not finding the slightest
resemblance in their habits as described by him, I gave the subject no further thought, considering the identity of such a bird a
myth. When some time afterwards, I mentioned the subject to
Mr. Enoch Stevens, who had removed from Darlington to the
Rondeau, he informed me that he not only remembered them
well, in his younger days, in Darlington, but had occasionally seen
them near his place, in the large woods at the Rondeau, and
promised when he returned, to send me a couple of specimens,
which in time, I duly received, and found to be (Hylotomus Pil-
eatus) or Peliated Woodpecker.

These woodpeckers were once quite plentiful through the woods
of the front Townships, but have long since retired to the inner
recesses of the more primeval forests. It is third in size to any
that is yet known. The largest of the species is the Mangrove
Woodpecker, of California; the second, the Ivory Billed Woodpecker, found on the Mississippi river, the third, the Pileated
Woodpecker, found in the most northern portions of Canada.
When seen flying, it is fully as large as a crow; it has a white
streak running down each side of the neck, and a red patch on
the top of the head.

The Gralatorial birds comprise the waders, and we find them
well represented in our locality. They inhabit the margin of rivers and lakes, while some are found in the tall grass and rushes,
that grow so abundantly in our marshes The Blue Heron is the
largest of the waders that visit us; it is found frequently in the
marshes, and nests in considerable numbers on Burr's Island,
Scugog Lake. Of the Bittern, we have two species, the American
Bittern, and the Least Bittern. The former is known also, as the
Indian Hen, Dunkadoo, and Stake Pounder. It may be heard
during the summer months, just before sunset, making a loud and
booming noise, which it repeats at regular intervals. Its flesh is
considered delicate and good.

The Plovers, Sandpipers, Curlews, Coots, and Water-Rails, also
belong to this order. Of the last group, we have three species :
the Virginia Rail, Clapper Rail, and Sora Rail, all of which, in

the Southern States, are highly esteemed on account of their delicate flavor. Here they are not generally known ; and as they possess the habit of skulking through the grass, and rushes, and can hardly be induced to take wing, even when not more than a few feet distant, they are not likely to come under the frequent notice of a casual observer. The Rails migrate during the night. They lay from four to five eggs, of a white ground color, speckled with light brown ; the nest is secreted in the thickest part of the rushes and bog, that cover our marshes

The Coot and Galinule are sometimes found in company with the rails. They are known to hunters by the name of Mud Hens, they breed in our marshes, and are polygamus in their habits, often three or four birds laying their eggs in the same nest. These are generally in the most conspicious places, but are so disguised that an inexperienced person would suppose, upon seeing one, that it never was intended for a nest, but was merely a pile of dead rushes, or rubbish, thrown promiscously together by the action of the water ; upon removing several layers of this material the eggs are found from six to seven inches below the surface.

Of the Wild Goose, we have only one species that visits us ; this is known as the Canada Goose, and passes regularly every spring on its way to the north, and in the autumn, it is again seen returning to the south, to spend the winter. This bird was found to be numerous in the early times in this part of Canada, and it was then usual to see large numbers of them feeding in the marshes and rivers. This, however, of late years has become a circumstance of very rare occurrence. Occasionally flocks are seen, and are immediately recognized by their peculiar form of flight, as well as by the continual hanking or clanking noise that they incessantly keep up ; but they are now no longer seen in large numbers feeding about our inland lakes and marshes, nor is this the only change that has taken place in reference to large aquatic birds. The Pelican and Swan were once numerous, and made their regular visits each spring and autumn, enlivening the bays and waters of this portion of Lake Ontario, but have long since ceased to make their appearance.

The Duck family embrace a large and varied class of very beautiful plumaged birds. Some of these have, in addition to their elegant markings and delicate tints, a showy crest, that can be raised or depressed at will; we have, in all, twenty-two different species of this family that visit this locality.

The whole of this class of birds are highly esteemed as an article of food, and are much sought after by gunners.   They, however, differ very much in point of excellence, some being so exceedingly delicious, juicy, and fine flavored, as to command a very high price in markets where they are known and appreciated ; as is the case with the Canvas Back Duck, which is allowed the precedence in point of flavor by all epicures, and readily sells for five or six dollars per pair in Baltimore or New York, while others are lean, dry and tough, and of doubtful taste.   Others again are of a decided fishy flavor, and can scarcely be eaten. As a general rule the wide billed birds should be chosen, and the narrow billed, especially the serated or sawbilled ones, should be rejected, as the latter live principally upon fish.

Among the wild duck, we find many gay and handsomely plumaged birds, but without doubt the Wood Duck (Aix Sponsa) is, by far, the most beautiful of all this group of birds.   The rich, changing lustre of its plumage is not surpassed by any duck in the world.   Unlike most other ducks, the Wood Duck builds its nest in a tree, from which it carries its young as soon as they are hatched, and places them in the water, which is usually close at hand.

The whole of the birds of North America comprise seven hundred and thirty-eight (738) different species.

ENTOMOLOGY.

The insects of this portion of Canada comprise a great many that are injurious to vegetation, some attack and destroy the trees of the forest, while others are ravaging upon the succulent plants and bulbous roots of the vegetable garden. Again, some are feeding upon the cereals and fruits, and others are destroying flowers and ornamental shrubs. Most of these pests are natives, but many of them have been imported along with foreign plants, or have migrated into the country, as is the case with the Colorado Beetle, which has proved so destructive to the potato crop; during the past few years. To many who have never made a study of insect life, it might at first appear very wonderful for those creatures to appear in such great numbers; but, on the contrary, to those who have made it a special study, it is but the fulfilment of a natural law. This insect was known by Entomologists to exist many years ago, in Colorado, and on the Upper Missouri River, when it fed upon a species of wild potato (Solanum Rostratum) which this animal found to be an equal, if not superior article of food to the wild species, thus following back in the wake of civilization, and finding an abundance of food in its onward march, it has multiplied and spread until it has completely inundated the country.

THE NEW COUNTRY.

BY AN OLD SETTLER, OVER 70 YEARS OF AGE.

In Darlington was my abode,
    Full seventy years ago;
And when good meat we wished to eat,
    We killed the buck or doe,
For fish we used the hook and line,
    And pounded corn to make it fine;
On Johnny Cake we used to dine,
    In the New Country.

Our occupation was to make
  The lofty forest bow ;
With axes good, we chopped the wood,
  For well we all knew how ,
We cleared the land for rye and wheat,
  For strangers and ourselves to eat ,
From maple trees we gathered sweet,
  In the New Country.

Our roads were winding through the woods,
  Where oft the savage trod ;
They were not wide, nor scarce a guide,
  But all the ones we had.
Our houses, too, were logs of wood,
  Rolled up in squares, and corked with mud ;
If the bark was tight, the roof was good,
  For a New Country.

The Indians ofttimes made us fear
  That there was danger nigh ;
The shaggy bear was ofttimes where
  The pig was, in his stye.
The savage wolves our children dread—
  Ofttimes our fearful mothers said,
Some beast of prey will take my babe,
  In the New Country.

We lived in social harmony,
  And drank the purling stream ;
No Lawyer, Priest, nor Doctor there,
  Was scarcely to be seen.
Our health it needed not repair—
  No pious man forgot his prayer—
And who could fee a lawyer there,
  In a New Country?

Of deerskins we made moccasins,
  To wear upon our feet ;
The checkered shirt was thought no hurt,
  Good company to keep.
And when a visit was to pay,
  On a winter's night, or winter's day,
The oxen drew the ladies' sleigh,
  In the New Country.

CPSIA information can be obtained
at www.ICGtesting.com
Printed in the USA
419549LV00009B/35